W9-CBC-810

PLANETS

MARS

Alexis Roumanis

LET'S READ
AV²
BY WEIGL™
ADDED VALUE • AUDIO VISUAL

Go to **www.av2books.com**, and enter this book's unique code.

BOOK CODE

Z637399

AV² by Weigl brings you media enhanced books that support active learning.

AV² provides enriched content that supplements and complements this book. Weigl's AV² books strive to create inspired learning and engage young minds in a total learning experience.

Your AV² Media Enhanced books come alive with...

Audio
Listen to sections of the book read aloud.

Video
Watch informative video clips.

Embedded Weblinks
Gain additional information for research.

Try This!
Complete activities and hands-on experiments.

Key Words
Study vocabulary, and complete a matching word activity.

Quizzes
Test your knowledge.

Slide Show
View images and captions, and prepare a presentation.

... and much, much more!

Published by AV² by Weigl
350 5th Avenue, 59th Floor New York, NY 10118
Websites: www.av2books.com   www.weigl.com

Library of Congress Cataloging-in-Publication Data

Roumanis, Alexis, author.
 Mars / Alexis Roumanis.
    pages cm. -- (Planets)
 Includes index.
 ISBN 978-1-4896-3288-3 (hard cover : alk. paper) -- ISBN 978-1-4896-3289-0 (soft cover : alk. paper) -- ISBN 978-1-4896-3290-6 (single user ebook) -- ISBN 978-1-4896-3291-3
(multi-user ebook)
 1. Mars (Planet)--Juvenile literature. I. Title.
 QB641.R675 2016
 523.43--dc23
                            2014041518

Printed in the United States of America in Brainerd, Minnesota
1 2 3 4 5 6 7 8 9 0   19 18 17 16 15

022015
WEP081214

Project Coordinator: Katie Gillespie Art Director: Terry Paulhus

Weigl acknowledges Getty Images and iStock as the primary image suppliers for this title.

MARS

CONTENTS

What Is Mars?

Mars is a planet. It moves in a path around the Sun. Mars is the fourth planet from the Sun.

Sun

Mercury

Venus

Earth

Mars

Ceres

Jupiter

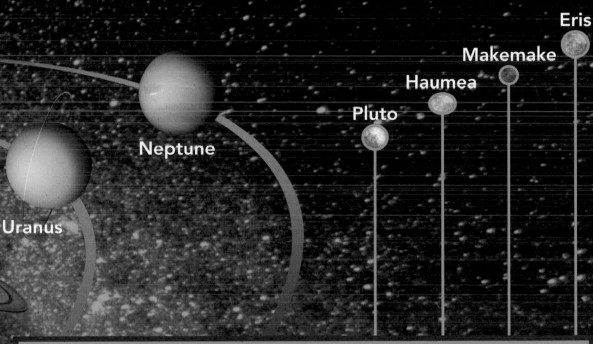

Eris

Makemake

Haumea

Pluto

Neptune

Uranus

Saturn

Dwarf Planets

Dwarf planets are round objects that move around the Sun. Unlike planets, they share their part of space with other objects.

How Big Is Mars?

Mars is the second smallest planet in the solar system. It is about half the size of Earth.

Earth

Mars

What Is Mars Made Of?

Mars is a rocky planet. It is made of rocks and metals. Mars is covered in a layer of dust.

9

10

What Does Mars Look Like?

Mars looks like a bright red star. It is sometimes called the Red Planet. Iron in the soil makes Mars look red.

What Is Olympus Mons?

Olympus Mons is a volcano on Mars. It is the highest known volcano in the solar system. Olympus Mons is more than twice as high as the tallest volcano on Earth.

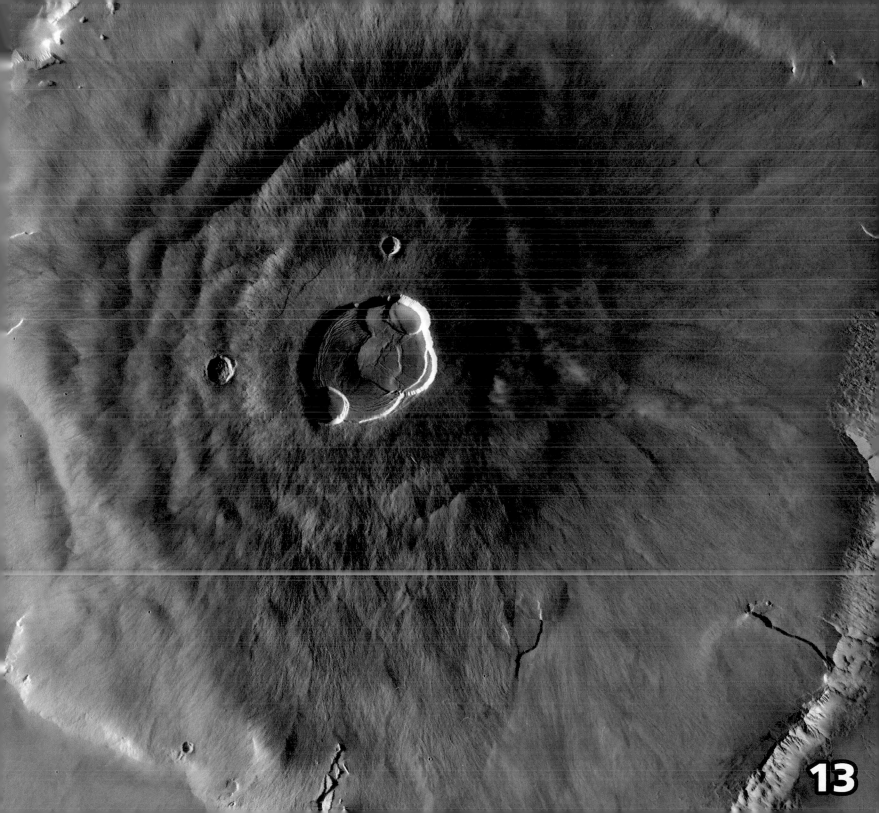

13

What Are Mars's Moons?

Mars has two moons. They are called Phobos and Deimos. Each moon is the size of a small town.

Phobos

Deimos

Who Named Mars?

The Ancient Romans thought Mars looked like the color of blood. They named the planet Mars after the god of war.

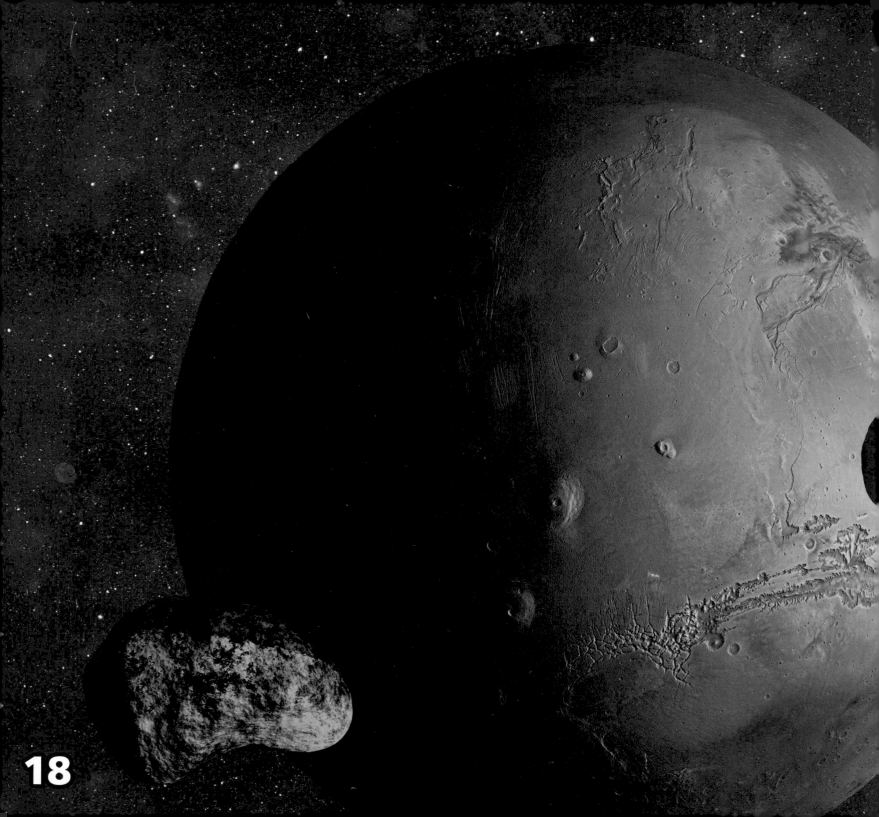

18

How Is Mars Different from Earth?

One day on Mars is about an hour longer than a day on Earth. One year on Mars is about twice as long as a year on Earth.

How Do We Learn about Mars Today?

Curiosity is a robot the same size as a car. It went to Mars in 2011 to study the planet. *Curiosity* is looking for signs of life on Mars.

MARS FACTS

This page provides more detail about the interesting facts found in the book. They are intended to be used by adults as a learning support to help young readers round out their knowledge of each planet featured in the *Planets* series.

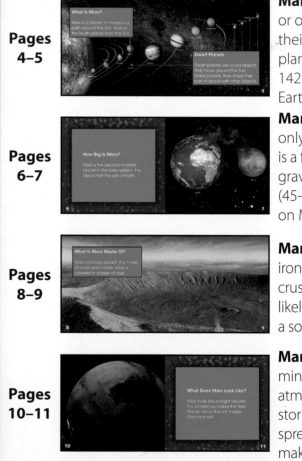

Pages 4–5

Mars is a planet. Planets are round objects that move around, or orbit, a star, with enough mass to clear smaller objects from their orbit. Earth's solar system has eight planets, five known dwarf planets, and many other space objects that all orbit the Sun. Mars is 142 million miles (229 million kilometers) from the Sun. It takes 687 Earth days for Mars to make one orbit around the Sun.

Pages 6–7

Mars is the second smallest planet in the solar system. It is only slightly larger than the largest moon in the solar system. Gravity is a force that pulls objects toward a planet's center. The force of gravity is much weaker on Mars than it is on Earth. A 100-pound (45-kilogram) object on Earth would only weigh 38 pounds (17 kg) on Mars.

Pages 8–9

Mars is a rocky planet. The surface of Mars is made up of rocks and iron dust. This dust is very fine. Underneath the dust, Mars has a rocky crust. It measures about 30 miles (50 km) thick. The center of Mars is likely made out of iron, nickel, and sulfur. Experts believe that Mars has a solid center, while Earth's core is both solid and liquid.

Pages 10–11

Mars looks like a bright red star. The soil on Mars is rich in iron minerals. As the iron minerals rust, they cause the soil to look red. An atmosphere is made up of gases that surround a planet. Powerful dust storms are common on Mars and can last for weeks. These dust storms spread iron minerals into the atmosphere. Dust in the atmosphere also makes the planet look red.

Olympus Mons is a volcano on Mars. Olympus Mons is 16 miles (25 km) in height and covers an area of 435 miles (700 km). The largest volcano on Earth is Mauna Loa in Hawai'i. Mauna Loa is only 6.3 miles (10 km) high and 75 miles (120 km) across. Volcanoes are larger on Mars than on Earth because the planet's crust does not move like the Earth's crust.

Mars has two moons. Mars's moons are two of the smallest moons in the solar system. The orbit of Phobos is only 3,700 miles (6,000 km) above Mars. This is the closest known orbit of any moon to its planet in the solar system. Phobos gets 5.9 feet (1.8 meters) closer to Mars each century. Scientists predict that Phobos may crash into Mars within 50 million years.

The Ancient Romans thought Mars looked like the color of blood. They named the planet after the god of war because of its deep red color. Mars was an important figure in Roman mythology, second only to Jupiter, king of the gods. Early astronomers in Egypt and China also named the planet after its color. In Egypt, they named it Her Desher, or "the red one." The Chinese name for Mars means "fire."

One day on Mars is about an hour longer than a day on Earth. All planets spin. This is called rotation. The time it takes for a planet to complete one rotation on its axis is the length of a day. This takes 24 hours on Earth, while a day on Mars is 24.6 hours, the smallest difference of any two planets in the solar system. However, a year on Mars is nearly twice as long as a year on Earth, since Mars is farther from the Sun than Earth.

Curiosity **is a robot the same size as a car.** It acts like a mobile laboratory. *Curiosity* can move around on the planet's surface, drill into rock, and collect rock samples. Special equipment can test what these samples are made from. *Curiosity* has found dried up rivers on Mars where water used to flow. It also helps study rock samples from Mount Sharp, which may be a good place to find past signs of life on Mars.

KEY WORDS

Research has shown that as much as 65 percent of all written material published in English is made up of 300 words. These 300 words cannot be taught using pictures or learned by sounding them out. They must be recognized by sight. This book contains 57 common sight words to help young readers improve their reading fluency and comprehension. This book also teaches young readers several important content words. These words are paired with pictures to aid in learning and improve understanding.

Page	Sight Words First Appearance
4	a, around, Earth, from, in, is, it, moves, the, what
5	are, of, other, part, that, their, they, with
6	about, big, how, second
8	and, made
11	does, like, looks, makes, sometimes
12	as, high, more, on, than
15	each, has, small, two
16	after, thought, who
19	an, day, different, long, one, year
21	car, do, for, learn, life, same, study, to, we, went

Page	Content Words First Appearance
4	Mars, path, planet, Sun
5	dwarf planets, objects, space
6	half, size, solar system
8	dust, layer, metals, rocks
11	iron, red, Red Planet, soil, star
12	Olympus Mons, twice, volcano
15	Deimos, moons, Phobos, town
16	Ancient Romans, blood, color, god, war
19	hour, twice
21	*Curiosity*, robot, signs, today